JOHN HARBISON

QUINTET FOR WINDS

Score

AMP 8028
Second edition: August 1999

ISBN 978-0-7935-1346-8

Associated Music Publishers, Inc.

DISTRIBUTED BY
HAL•LEONARD® CORPORATION
7777 W. BLUEMOUND RD. P.O. BOX 13819 MILWAUKEE, WI 53213

PROGRAM NOTE

Quintet for Winds was composed in the summer of 1978 for the Aulos Quintet, on commission from the Naumburg Foundation. The piece has been performed by many groups—most notably the Emmanuel Wind Quintet, who have performed it over 40 times and gave the first New York City performance in 1980.

The piece especially emphasizes mixtures and doublings and maintains a classically simple surface. It is extremely challenging to play, and one of the principal rewards of the piece has been the opportunity to work with a number of resourceful, inquisitive, and fearless wind players in the mutually beneficial expansion of their repertory.

—John Harbison

first performance:
Aulos Wind Quintet
April 15, 1979, in Jordan Hall, Boston

recordings:
Aulos Wind Quintet, CRI SD 436
Arioso Wind Quintet, Koch 3-7262-2
Reykjavik Wind Quintet, Chandos CHAN 9174

duration: ca. 23 minutes

QUINTET FOR WINDS

I. Intrada

John Harbison
(1978)

Poco più mosso (𝅗𝅥 = 69)
13
ff
18
sf
rit.
23
a tempo
mp, pieno
p
mf
mp

28
mp
mp
sfp
sf
p
mf
mp
mp
mf
mp
mf
33
poco animando
mf
mp
3
cresc.
f, marc.
38
poco più mosso
f
ff
cresc.

43
rit.

49
a tempo
mf
mp
f
mp
p

54
poco più mosso
a tempo
ff
mf
sf

animando
poco più mosso
a tempo
59
cresc.
ff
sf
mf
movendo
64
p
cresc.
mf
calando, ritardando
68
f
dim. molto
dim.
pp

72
poco più mosso
ff
sf
77
f
ff
82
pressando

poco rit.
86
ff
f
Risoluto, meno mosso
(𝅗𝅥 = 66)
90
ff
f
94
ff
f
sf

II. Intermezzo

Allegretto, lusingando

♩ = 90

12
cedendo
a tempo
legato
17
dim.
22
rit.
a tempo

27
cresc.
f
p, subito
32
rit.
cresc.
mf
mp
f
37
a tempo
p, grazioso
p

41
45
pp
pp
pp
pp
49
cresc.
cresc.
cresc.
cresc.
p
p
p
p
tr
cresc.
cresc.
cresc.
mp
mp

53
mp
tr
cresc.
mf
p
57
61
cresc.

65
mp
cresc.
69
mf
mfp
cresc.
73
dim.
fp

III. Romanza

Andante ♩ = 76–80

ritardando molto *a tempo*

molto rit.

a tempo
pp, dolce
animando
rallentando
mf cantabile
cresc.
a tempo
pp, dolce

24
molto animando
mf, legato
cresc.
28
molto rit.
a tempo
32

37
42
47

52
56
poco animando
61
G. P.
quasi a tempo,
poco meno mosso

66
movendo
a tempo
72
molto
76
animando
poco più mosso
cresc.
f molto
f molto
f molto

79
molto rit.
a tempo
pp, cantibile
84
cresc.
88
cresc.
f molto

animando
Più mosso (𝅗𝅥 = 92)
cresc.

105
molto rit.
lunga
a tempo
111
117
rit.
poco meno mosso
poco rit.

IV. Scherzo

Prestissimo 𝅗𝅥. = 90

31
f
f
f
f
f
sf
sf
37
ff sf
f
ff
ff
sf
f
ff
ff
43
mf
mf
mf
mf

49
mf
mf
55
mf
mf
61
f
ff
f
ff sf
f
ff
ff
sf
ff
ff

67
sf
sf
73
ff
79
G. P.
Moderato, rubato
poco rit.
f, intenso
f, intenso
f, intenso
f, intenso

85
a tempo, movendo
più animato
ritardando
sf
sf
sf
sf
92
a tempo
poco movendo
rallentando
sf
sf
sf
sf
mp
mp
mp
mp
98
Tempo I, prestissimo
ff
sf
ff
ff
ff
ff

104
f
f
f
f
110
mf
mf
mf
mf
116
mf
mf

140
146
152

158
mf
f
164
mf
f
(>)
170
ff
sfz

V. Finale

Adagio 𝅗𝅥 **= 54**

15
G.P.
p
pp
al sord.
21
Alla marcia, ♩ = 108
f, staccatissimo
f, ruvido
con sord.
24
frullato
ff

* Horn and oboe may omit the notes in brackets to take a rest. The clarinet should play if these rests are taken.

36
cresc.
40
via sord.
43
poco rit.

a tempo
47
fpp
fpp
p
p
fp
fmp, agitato
p, agitato
aperto senza sord.
p, agitato
mp, agitato
fp
50
1.
2.
pp
f
cresc.
mf
mf
cresc.
mf
sf
f
al sord.
al sord.
cresc.
mf
mf
cresc.
mf
sf
f
53
pp
pp
p
p
pp
p
con sord.
ff, staccatissimo
pp
p

58
mp
mf
f
62
cresc.
ff
via sord.
66

69
amoroso
pp staccatissimo, giocoso
staccatissimo
aperto
senza sord.
staccatissimo
72
75
p staccatissimo

78
mp
mp
p
p
p
pp
pp
dim.
dim.
pp
dim.
82
pp in rilievo
pp
ppp
pp
ppp
al sord.
pp
pp
molto
86
f, ruvido
f, staccatissimo
f, ruvido
con sord.
f, staccatissimo
f, staccatissimo
sf
sf
sf
sf
sf
sf

89
cresc.
cresc.
cresc.
cresc.
cresc.
92
ff
f
ff
95
poco meno mosso
mp
tr
f
mp , poco stacc.
cresc.

99
cresc.
p, troppo dolce (esagerato)
via sord.
p, poco stacc.
103
mp troppo dolce (esagerato)
mp troppo dolce (esagerato)
senza sord.
106
(movendo)
a tempo
cresc.
mf agitato
mf agitato

109
f, agitato
f, agitato
f, agitato
f, agitato
ff
ff
ff
ff
112
f
f
f
ff
fp
fp
f sf
sf
ff
fp
fp
f sf
sf
115
cresc.
cresc.
cresc.
cresc.
cresc.
ff sf
f
sf
ff sf
sf
ff sf
f
sf
ff sf
f
sf
ff sf
f
sf

118
121
124

127
129
pressando
8va
sf
ff
gliss.
132
8
loco
mf

JOHN HARBISON

QUINTET FOR WINDS

Flute

AMP 8028
Second edition: August 1999

ISBN 978-0-7935-1346-8

Associated Music Publishers, Inc.

DISTRIBUTED BY
HAL•LEONARD®
CORPORATION
7777 W. BLUEMOUND RD. P.O. BOX 13819 MILWAUKEE, WI 53213

FLUTE

QUINTET FOR WINDS

I. Intrada

John Harbison
(1978)

51
mp
f
mp
p
poco più mosso
ff
a tempo
mf
sf
57
sf
animando
cresc.
poco più mosso
ff
sf
62
a tempo
mf
p
cresc.
66
mf
movendo
cresc.
f
calando,
ritardando
dim. molto
70
pp
poco più mosso
ff
sf
76
sf
f
ff
f
81
ff
f
85
pressando
ff
poco rit.
f
Risoluto, meno mosso
(𝅗𝅥 = 66)
89
ff
f
94
ff
f
ff
sf

II. Intermezzo

44
pp
49
cresc.
p
cresc.
53
cresc.
mf
p
57
61
cresc.
65
mp
cresc.
69
mf
73
dim.
mp
dim.
fp

III. Romanza

Andante ♩ = 76–80
ritard. molto
a tempo
molto rit.
mp
Cl.
a tempo
p
pp
pp, dolce
animando rallentando
mf
mf
p
a tempo
pp, dolce
mp
pp
molto animando
mf
mp
f
mp
cresc.
molto rit.
a tempo
mf
p
pp
f
sf
f
sf
sf
ff
sf
f
sf
sf
sf
sf
sf
sf
ff
p
f
p

poco animando
G. P.
quasi a tempo,
poco meno mosso
movendo
a tempo
animando
poco più mosso
Ob.
molto rit.
a tempo
animando
cresc.
Più mosso (♩ = 92)
molto rit.
lunga
a tempo
rit.
poco meno mosso
poco rit.

IV. Scherzo

Moderato, rubato
Ob.
poco rit.
a tempo, movendo
più animato
ritardando
a tempo
poco movendo
rallentando
Tempo I, prestissimo
Ob.
ff
sf
f
mf
ffsf
sf
ff

V. Finale

Adagio 𝅗𝅥 = 54
pp p sf pp mp sf p sf sf mp
G. P.
Cl.
11
p pp
G.P.
Alla marcia, ♩ = 108
21
2
Cl.
27
frullato
f ff f, ruvido sf
31
cresc.
34
poco meno mosso
frullato
ff mf ff mp mf
39
ff mp f mf
43
mp
46
poco rit.
a tempo
mf fpp p fp
51
1.
2.
tr
pp f pp p

cresc.
amoroso
pp in rilievo
f, ruvido
cresc.

poco meno mosso
mp
f mp
f mp< mf
mp
3
mp troppo dolce (esagerato)
p
(movendo) a tempo
mp cresc.
mf
cresc.
f, agitato
ff
f
cresc.
ffsf
f
sf
ff
sf f
sf
sf
ff
pressando
sf
8va
sf
loco
mf

JOHN HARBISON

QUINTET FOR WINDS

Oboe

AMP 8028

Second edition: August 1999

ISBN 978-0-7935-1346-8

Associated Music Publishers, Inc.

DISTRIBUTED BY
HAL•LEONARD®
CORPORATION
7777 W. BLUEMOUND RD. P.O. BOX 13819 MILWAUKEE, WI 53213

OBOE

QUINTET FOR WINDS

I. Intrada

John Harbison
(1978)

poco più mosso
a tempo
ff
mf
sf
sf
animando
poco più mosso
a tempo
cresc.
ff
sf
mf
movendo
mf
cresc.
calando, ritardando
poco più mosso
f
dim.
ff
sf
sf
f
ff
f
pressando
ff
f
Risoluto, meno mosso (𝅗𝅥 = 66)
poco rit.
ff
f
ff
f
ff
f
ff
sf

II. Intermezzo

44
pp
49
cresc.
p
cresc.
mp
54
p
59
63
cresc.
mp
69
mf
73
dim.
mp
dim.
fp

III. Romanza

Andante ♩ = 76–80
ritardando molto
a tempo
molto rit.
a tempo
8
animando
rallentando
a tempo
Fl.
pp, dolce
mf, legato
molto animando
cresc.
molto rit.
a tempo
poco animando

63
G. P.
quasi a tempo,
poco meno mosso
ff
Cl.
pp mp
70
movendo
a tempo
animando
p mf p mp mf p
78
poco più mosso
molto rit.
a tempo
5
f molto
mf p
Hn.
88
mp
cresc.
f molto
93
animando
sf sf sf
97
Più mosso (♩ = 92)
sf cresc.
ff
101
sf sf sf sf sf sf sf sf
106
molto rit.
lunga
a tempo
2
sf sf mp
p < mp > pp
p < mp
114
2
rit.
poco meno mosso
poco rit.
pp
Fl.
p

IV. Scherzo

Prestissimo 𝅗𝅥. = 90
Cl.
G. P.
f, intenso
Moderato, rubato
poco rit.
a tempo, movendo
più animato

90
ritardando
a tempo
poco
movendo
rallentando
sf
mp
Tempo I, prestissimo
98
7
Cl.
ff
111
6
mf
123
3
f
ff
mf
133
f
141
3
mf
151
158
f
167
ff

V. Finale

* Oboe may omit the notes in brackets to take a rest. The clarinet should play if this rest is taken.

staccatissimo, giocoso
cresc.
f, staccatissimo
cresc.
poco meno mosso

99
mp < mf
mp
p, troppo dolce (esagerato)
104
(movendo) a tempo
mp troppo dolce (esagerato)
p
mp
cresc.
mf
cresc.
109
f, agitato
ff
f
113
cresc.
ff sf
117
sf
ff
120
sf
f sf
sf
sf
sf
sf
124
ff
127
pressando
130
sf
sf
sf
mf

JOHN HARBISON

QUINTET FOR WINDS

Clarinet in B♭

AMP 8028
Second edition: August 1999

ISBN 978-0-7935-1346-8

Associated Music Publishers, Inc.
Distributed by
HAL•LEONARD® CORPORATION
7777 W. Bluemound Rd. P.O. Box 13819 Milwaukee, WI 53213

CLARINET IN B♭

QUINTET FOR WINDS

I. Intrada

John Harbison
(1978)

56
a tempo
sf
sf
animando
cresc.
60
poco più mosso
ff
sf
a tempo
mf
p
65
cresc.
mf
movendo
cresc.
68
calando, ritardando
f
dim. molto
pp
72
poco più mosso
ff
sf
sf
78
f
ff
f
82
ff
f
pressando
86
poco rit.
ff
f
Risoluto, meno mosso (𝅗𝅥 = 66)
90
ff
f
ff
95
f
ff
sf

II. Intermezzo

39
45
pp
cresc.
p
51
tr
cresc.
mp
tr
cresc.
mf
56
p
62
cresc.
mp
67
cresc.
mfp
cresc.
71
mf
dim.
mp
fp

III. Romanza

Andante ♩ = 76–80

55
poco animando
61
G. P.
quasi a tempo,
poco meno mosso
67
movendo
a tempo
73
animando
molto
cresc.
f molto
78
poco più mosso
molto rit.
a tempo
87
cresc.
cresc.
94
animando
cresc.
98
Più mosso (♩ = 92)
102
107
molto rit.
lunga
a tempo
115
rit.
poco meno mosso
poco rit.

IV. Scherzo

Moderato, rubato
poco rit.
a tempo, movendo
G. P.
f, intenso
più animato
ritardando
a tempo
poco movendo
rallentando
Tempo I, prestissimo

120
7
ff
sfp
mp
mf
133
138
3
f
sf
146
sf
mf
151
sfp
mf
156
sfp
mf
161
f
mf
167
f
ff

V. Finale

* Horn and oboe may omit the notes in brackets to take a rest. The clarinet should play if these rests are taken.

41
mf
44
mp
poco rit.
mf
47
a tempo
p, agitato
tr
cresc.
51
1.
2.
mf
sf
f
pp
56
p
mp
mf
f
62
cresc.
ff
6
65
3
68
sf
staccatissimo
p
72
2

dim.
f, ruvido
cresc.
poco meno mosso
mp, poco stacc.
cresc.
cresc.
mp p, troppo dolce (esagerato)
(movendo) a tempo
mf agitato
cresc.
f, agitato

cresc.
pressando

JOHN HARBISON

QUINTET FOR WINDS

Horn in F

AMP 8028
Second edition: August 1999

ISBN 978-0-7935-1346-8

Associated Music Publishers, Inc.

DISTRIBUTED BY
HAL•LEONARD® CORPORATION
7777 W. BLUEMOUND RD. P.O. BOX 13819 MILWAUKEE, WI 53213

HORN IN F

QUINTET FOR WINDS

I. Intrada

John Harbison
(1978)

animando
poco più mosso
a tempo
cresc.
movendo
calando, ritardando
dim. molto
poco più mosso
pressando
Risoluto, meno mosso (𝅗𝅥 = 66)
poco rit.

II. Intermezzo

III. Romanza

Andante ♩ = 76–80
ritard. molto
a tempo
ppp
mp
p
mp
mf
p
mf
Cl.
molto rit.
a tempo
Fl.
pp
2
mp
animando
rallentando
a tempo
mf cantabile
cresc.
f
p
pp
molto animando
molto rit.
a tempo
f
sf
ff
mf
p
ff

58
poco animando
63
G. P.
quasi a tempo,
poco meno mosso
70
movendo
a tempo
76
animando
poco più mosso
molto rit.
82
a tempo
pp, cantibile
86
cresc.
91
animando
Più mosso (♩ = 92)
97
cresc.
105
molto rit.
lunga
a tempo
114
rit.
poco meno mosso
poco rit.

IV. Scherzo

Prestissimo 𝅗𝅥. = 90
f
mf
Cl.
mf
f
ff
mf
mf
ff
G. P.
Moderato, rubato
𝅗𝅥. = ♩
f, intenso
poco rit.
a tempo, movendo
più animato
ritardando
sf

a tempo
poco movendo
rallentando
Tempo I, prestissimo

V. Finale

* Horn may omit the notes in brackets to take a rest. The clarinet should play if this rest is taken.

via sord.
cresc.
ff
senza sord.
aperto
ffsf
p staccatissimo
mp
p
dim.
pp
al sord.
con sord.
f, staccatissimo
cresc.
poco meno mosso
via sord.
senza sord.
mf
(movendo)
a tempo
mf agitato
fp
fsf
sf
f
ffsf
pressando
Fl.
gliss.

JOHN HARBISON

QUINTET FOR WINDS

Bassoon

AMP 8028
Second edition: August 1999

ISBN 978-0-7935-1346-8

Associated Music Publishers, Inc.

DISTRIBUTED BY
HAL•LEONARD®
CORPORATION
7777 W. BLUEMOUND RD. P.O. BOX 13819 MILWAUKEE, WI 53213

BASSOON

QUINTET FOR WINDS

I. Intrada

John Harbison
(1978)

Moderato 𝅗𝅥 = 60 – 63
comminciando lentamente, movendo
mp, pieno
a tempo
mf
calando
meno mosso
movendo
p
Poco più mosso (𝅗𝅥 = 69)
f
ff
rit.
a tempo
sf
sf > mp
p
mf
mp < mf > mp
poco animando
cresc.
f, marc.
poco più mosso
cresc.
ff
rit.
a tempo
mf
mp
f > mp > p
poco più mosso
ff

Copyright © 1979 by Associated Music Publishers (BMI) New York, NY
International Copyright Secured. All Rights Reserved.
Warning: Unauthorized reproduction of this publication is prohibited by Federal law and subject to criminal prosecution.

55
a tempo
mf
sf
sf
59
animando
poco più mosso
ff
sf
a tempo
mf
64
p
cresc.
mf
movendo
2
calando, ritardando
3
72
poco più mosso
ff
sf
sf
sf
78
f
ff
f
82
ff
f
pressando
Risoluto, meno mosso (𝅗𝅥 = 66)
86
ff
poco rit.
f
90
ff
f
ff
95
f
ff
sf

II. Intermezzo

Allegretto, lusingando

♩ = 90

III. Romanza

Andante ♩ = 76–80
ritard. molto
a tempo
molto rit.
a tempo
animando
rallentando
a tempo
cresc.
molto animando
molto rit.
cresc.
a tempo
poco animando
G. P.

quasi a tempo,
poco meno mosso
65
ppp
movendo
a tempo
p
mf
72
mp
mf
3
f
tr
mf
f sf
animando
f molto
5
6
poco più mosso
78
f
mf
molto rit.
a tempo
p pp
3
84
p
mp
mf
88
cresc.
f sf
sf
94
animando
sf
sf cresc. sf
ff sf
Più mosso (♩ = 92)
101
molto rit.
mf
108
lunga
a tempo
ppp
p < mp > pp
116
p
rit.
sf mp
poco meno mosso
poco rit.

IV. Scherzo

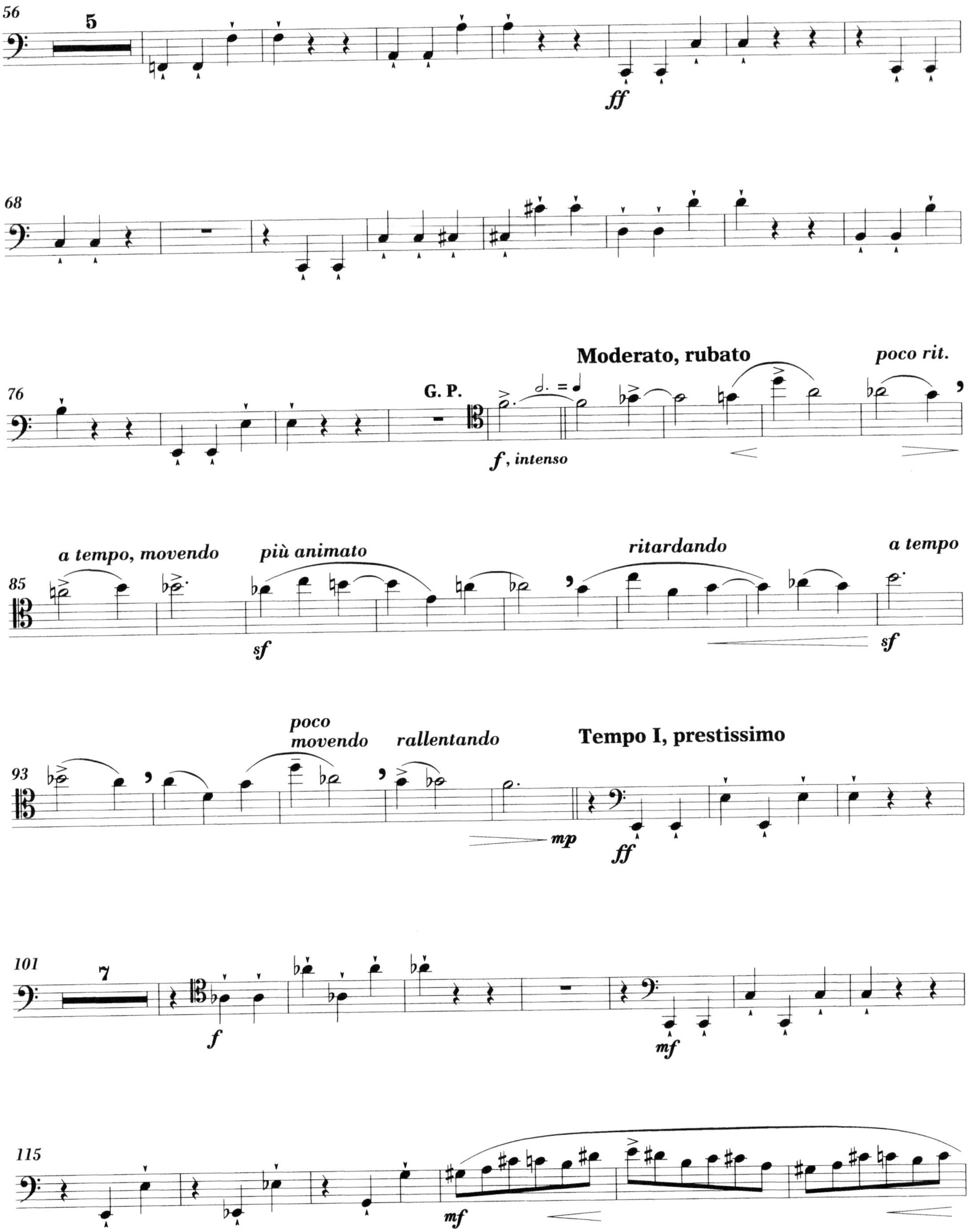
Moderato, rubato
poco rit.
G. P.
f, intenso
a tempo, movendo
più animato
ritardando
a tempo
poco movendo
rallentando
Tempo I, prestissimo

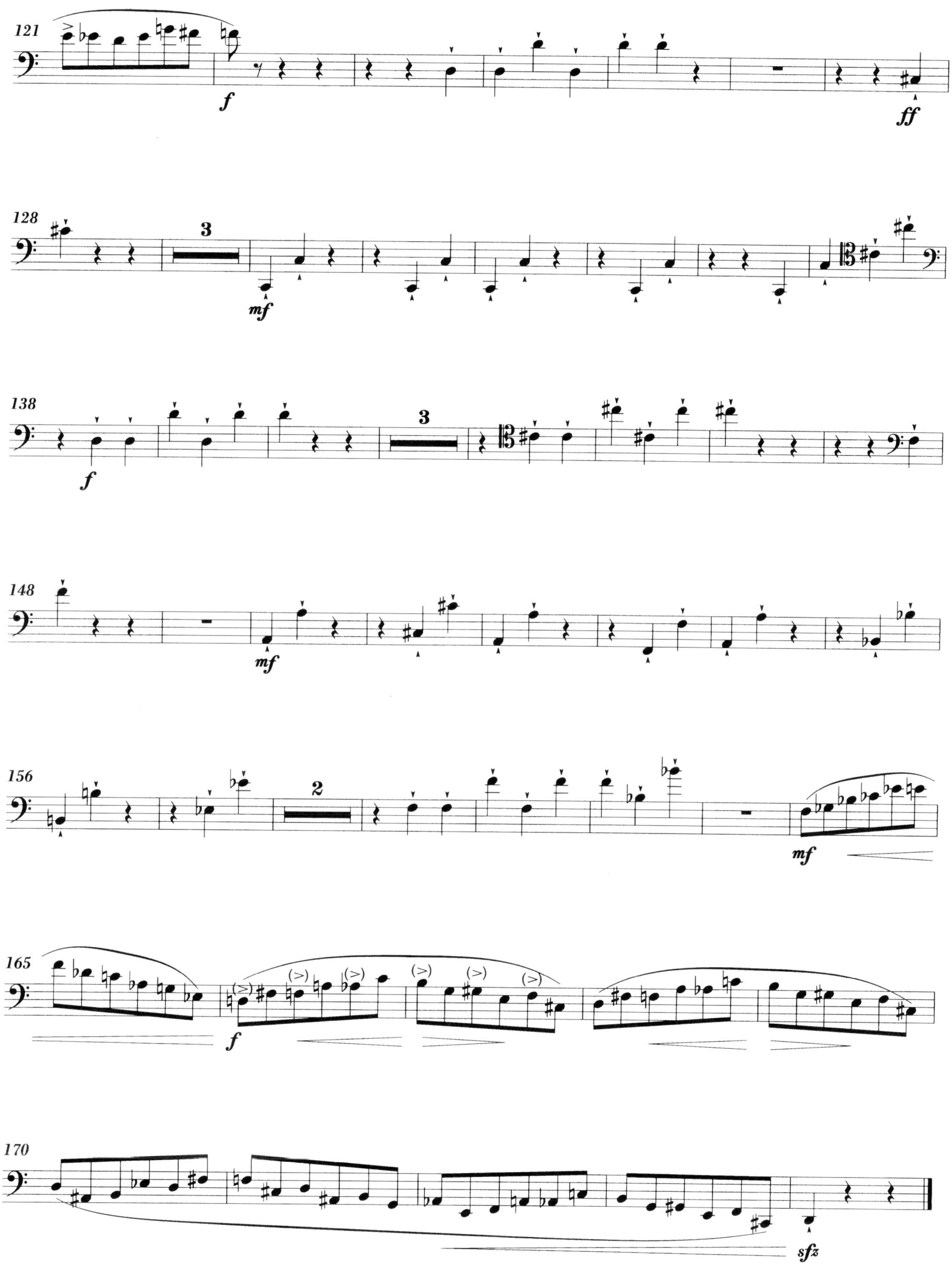
121
f
ff
128
3
mf
138
f
3
148
mf
156
2
mf
165
f
170
sfz

V. Finale

Adagio 𝅗𝅥 = 54
G. P.
pp p sf
pp mp sf
p sf
mp sf
pp
f
p f
mp, sost.
p
G.P.
Alla marcia, ♩ = 108
pp
f, staccatissimo
cresc.
ff
poco meno mosso
mf
poco staccato
cresc.
ff
mp
mf
cresc.
ff
f
mf
poco rit.
a tempo
2
fp
cresc.
1.
2.
mf
sf
f

53
60
cresc.
65
68
staccatissimo
72
77
dim.
82
molto
f, staccatissimo
87
cresc.
93
poco meno mosso
3

Cl.
p, poco stacc.
(movendo)
a tempo
cresc.
f, agitato
pressando